THE little
HASTINGS
FISH
COOK BOOK

Dedicated to the memory of
Elspeth Thompson 1961 – 2010
with our love

FIRST EDITION
PUBLISHED 2009
SECOND EDITION
PUBLISHED 2010
THIRD EDITION
PUBLISHED 2010

ISBN 978-0-9563663-0-6

© Sea Saw Books
West Villa 1 Victoria Road St Leonards on Sea
East Sussex TN37 6ER

THE little HASTINGS FISH COOK BOOK

SALLY WALTON

Illustrations by Stewart Walton
Design by Debi Angel

SAW
books

1 2 3 4

WINKLE ISLAND

ROCK-A-NORE

BEACH

N

W   E

S

8
12

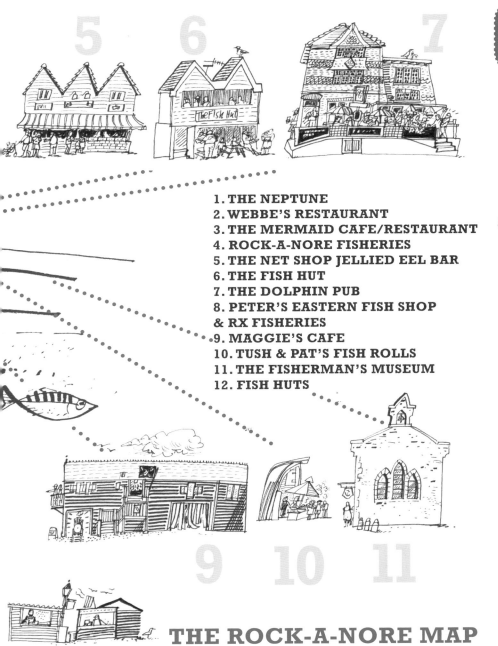

1. THE NEPTUNE
2. WEBBE'S RESTAURANT
3. THE MERMAID CAFE/RESTAURANT
4. ROCK-A-NORE FISHERIES
5. THE NET SHOP JELLIED EEL BAR
6. THE FISH HUT
7. THE DOLPHIN PUB
8. PETER'S EASTERN FISH SHOP
   & RX FISHERIES
9. MAGGIE'S CAFE
10. TUSH & PAT'S FISH ROLLS
11. THE FISHERMAN'S MUSEUM
12. FISH HUTS

5

THE ROCK-A-NORE MAP

The Hastings Fishing Fleet

Small fishing boats have been putting out to sea
from Hastings for over a thousand years and their
way of fishing has hardly changed in all that time.
Living here we are privileged to be able to watch
the boats go out, then buy the fresh catch a few
paces from where it is landed. We witness how
hard it can be to work from an open boat in all
weathers, setting off from the shingle and
hauling the boats back up with the help of
the Boys Ashore. It is their whole life, not
just a job and we must all support our local
fishing industry which has one of the most
environmentally friendly fleets in the country.

Our fishmongers on the Stade are
world-class and the day's local
catch can also be bought from
the fishing huts on the beach.
And for those who can't wait
there is one of Tush & Pat's
Fish Rolls – 2 crispy fillets
of the day's fresh catch
cooked in olive oil under a brolly
by the net huts – it hits the spot!

The Hastings Fleet has Marine Stewardship
Council Certification for its Dover Sole,
Mackerel and Herring. This global,
not-for-profit organisation aims to solve the
problem of over-fishing by harnessing
consumer-power. By choosing fish with the
blue and white MSC logo we show our support
for the environment and our respect for the
fishermen, who by their sustainable fishing
methods help to maintain the balance of nature.

This book is dedicated to these local heroes.

A very BIG thanks to everyone who answered the call. This is your book too....

Lois Waldron, Marianne Smith, Maggie Alderson, Jilly Sillem, Jane Scruton, Craig Sams, Pam Smith, Samara Streeten, Sharon Bartlett, Sonny, Dex & Gail, Kathryn Flett, Roo Walton, Michael Foster MP, Maureen Charlesworth, Ben Krikorian/Dragon Bar, Jamie Stephens/Pomegranate, Elspeth Thompson, John Cole, Louise Bell, Lesley/Aardvark, Sharon Bigg, Spike Smilgin, Jan Baldwin, Diana Holubowitz, Old Town Deli Mobile Catering, Lisa & Emmanuel/Judges, Alastair Fairley, Lesley/Blackrock House, Tony Howard, Mark Storr-Hoggins & Dave Watkins LOCKSMITH

Thanks to The Chefs

RICK STEIN is the UK's most famous man of fish and promoter of local food and also a good friend to Hastings. He has visited many times and featured our local fishermen on his TV programmes. We are very proud to have been given one of his recipes for our book.

TOM AIKENS is a highly successful chef/patron who made a guest appearance at Hastings Seafood & Wine Festival in 2008. He was instantly generous when asked for a recipe and gave us four to choose from.

NICK HALES spent 16 years working in fine London restaurants before moving to Hastings and opening one of his own. St Clements in St Leonards on Sea is in the Michelin Guide and Nick always has the best of the day's local catch on the menu.

ALASTAIR HENDY cooks, photographs and writes about food. Having completed the restoration of his Tudor house in All Saints Street he will be running a fish cookery school and opening a Homewares shop in the Old Town High Street.

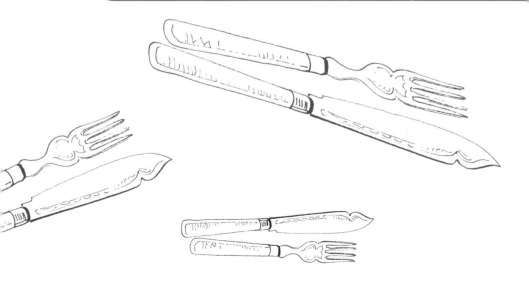

"What fish shall we eat today?"

"What herb was in that dish yesterday?"

"Remember that salad we ate on the East Hill picnic ?"

"How does Craig do his mackerel?"

"What was that delicious pie we had on Leo's birthday?"

Author's Note
We have dreamed about this little book for quite a long time. When we met Debi it somehow all clicked into place and Sea Saw Books was born. I have tried to use all the recipes as they were sent but some have had to be trimmed down due to lack of space. I hope that I have stayed true to the essence of your contribution. Nothing will be wasted and all the extra recipes and mouth - watering descriptions are in the 'stock pot' for the next book. I have added some of our own favourites to balance out the fish varieties and these are marked with a little fish.

This book was born out of our curiosity and greed – we loved the different ways people in Hastings cook fish and wanted to try it again ourselves, perhaps with a bit more spice or with a different accompaniment.
We asked friends, fishmongers and chefs to send us their favourites with the proviso that they must include the most sustainable of the local catch.

The recipes appear as written and donated and we hope you enjoy the rich variety of styles.

We want to be more experimental when buying fish. It's all too easy to buy what's familiar, and far more interesting to ask questions and try new flavours.
Let's all shop inquisitively everyday, as if we were on holiday.

COATING FISH FOR FRYING

If fish is to be fried it is always best to coat it to form a barrier between the hot fat and the skin or flesh. This can be as simple as dusting it with flour but you can also add flavour with additional coatings. Always begin with seasoned flour – a generous addition of salt and pepper will improve the flavour, especially when the fish is fried in butter. For a nice crisp coating, dust the fish with flour then dip in beaten egg then flour again.

FRESH BREADCRUMBS:

Place the breadcrumbs in a food processor or blender and whizz till the lumps disappear. Make sure the oil is hot when you add the fish, otherwise the soft crumbs will absorb it, become heavy and drop off.

DRIED BREADCRUMBS:

Break stale bread into chunks and dry slowly in an oven set to a low temperature. You want to remove the moisture but not cook the bread. Once dry and light put them in a blender and whizz until they have a fine and even texture.

POLENTA (CORNMEAL):

Polenta makes a crunchy corn flavoured coating. Nice with salsa!

OATMEAL:

This is a traditional coating for herrings in Scotland and is just as good for other oily fish like mackerel or sardines. Dip the fish in milk then oatmeal. It will absorb the oiliness and develop a nutty flavour when fried to a crisp. Suggested flavours to add to coatings: fresh herbs; grated Parmesan; cayenne pepper; smoked paprika

BEER BATTER:

200g SR white flour
330ml cold lager
pinch of sea salt.
This makes a good basic fish frying batter.
Sift the flour into a bowl and pour in the lager, whisking until you have a smooth batter with the consistency of double cream. Dry the fish then coat it with batter and deep fry.

TEMPURA:

A Japanese ultra-light batter.
250ml iced fizzy water
125g white SR flour
Whisk the batter ingredients lightly with a chopstick and use it straight away. Lumpy is fine!
Tip: Tempura packet mix is brilliant!

FISH STOCK
or COURT BOULLION

When the fishmonger fillets your fish ask him to give you a bag of bones, heads and tails. Rinse under a cold tap and put in a pot. Cover with water and boil then skim off any scum that forms on the surface.

Add a peeled sliced onion, a clove or two of garlic, parsley with stalks and a bay leaf.

Simmer for 25 minutes and strain.

To freeze: **Boil hard to reduce the stock by half then freeze in ice cube trays.**

Once frozen the cubes can be bagged up and labelled. Use a couple at a time to add flavour to any fish stew or sauce.

Tip

Try different species of fish that you may not have had before, ie mackerel, sardines, red mullet, prawns – all these fish are great pre-cooked for picnics. *Tom Aikens*

OILS: The most vital thing is to use fresh oil when frying fish. Oil absorbs and retains flavours. Strained oil is okay for re-use several times for chips but *not* for fish and never for marinades or salads.

GROUNDNUT
This is a light coloured and tasteless oil. When you want the mild or subtle flavour of the fish to shine through.
Most used in Chinese recipes.

LIGHT OLIVE
Best for frying. Gives a distinctive olive flavour so is good for Mediterranean style fish.

SOYA
Made from soya beans. It has no distinct flavour.

VIRGIN OLIVE
Not ideal for frying but great for salads or marinades.

VEGETABLE
Made from a mixture of plant sources – mostly soya oil. It is the cheapest cooking oil and it will fry things!

SUNFLOWER
All purpose cooking oil with a golden colour. Made from crushed sunflower seeds. Good for fish and chips.

RAPE SEED
Recommended for low cholesterol diets. It is worth buying unrefined organic oil for its strong colour and nutty flavour.

SESAME
It has a very strong flavour and is best diluted with groundnut oil. Use this for Chinese or Japanese style recipes.

BUTTER
Fish fried in butter is delicious. Use it for sole or very fresh plaice fillets. Adding a small amount of oil will prevent the butter burning.

LARD
Traditionally used to fry chips up north. Aficionados say there is no better way!

13

Tip

Particularly in the summer, it's nice to have fish on a BBQ. Any fish or shellfish is best marinated before it goes on the BBQ as it will give it extra flavour. *Tom Aikens*

SOME VEGETABLE IDEAS

MUSHY PEAS

A softie Southern version of the Northern standard. Take a 450g packet of frozen peas, add salt, pepper, a small cup of chicken stock, a big squeeze of lemon and a handful of fresh mint.
Boil for 5 minutes then blend for a half a minute or less so the peas turn to a mush but not a puree. Serve with fish and chips.

GRATED COURGETTE

Grate a courgette or two, sprinkle with salt and leave to drain in a colander for half an hour. Wash under a cold tap and dry in kitchen paper or a clean tea towel squeezing out the moisture.
Melt a knob of butter in a pan and gently fry a clove of crushed garlic then add the courgette and stir it into the garlicky butter. Cook for a few minutes then serve spoonfuls with grilled fish.

MASHED POTATO WITH LEMON ZEST

Peel and boil floury potatoes then mash with butter and season as usual. Add the finely grated rind of one unwaxed lemon. Lovely with pan-fried, roasted or grilled fish.

THAI-STYLE CUCUMBER SALAD

Peel a cucumber and slice it lengthways into sticks, removing the seeds. Put into a bowl and cover with 2 chopped shallots or a small chopped red onion and a red chilli cut in fine rounds.
Mix up a dressing from 1 cup of rice or white wine vinegar, half a cup of water, half a cup of sugar, a pinch of ground turmeric and a crushed garlic clove.
Heat these together in a small pan until the sugar dissolves, then pour the mixture over the cucumber. Chill to serve. This will keep in the fridge in a glass jar for two weeks.

SAMPHIRE

We are so lucky in Hastings because samphire grows locally and is on sale at the fishmongers. It's succulent and salty and the perfect accompaniment to local fish. It's versatile too. Eat it raw or steamed. We add it to salads or stir-fry it in butter with garlic. There are no rules so enjoy experimenting with this gift from the marshes.

Tip

SAMPHIRE is on sale from May till August Pour a kettle of boiling water over it then drain and eat with butter and black pepper.

Gail at Rock a Nore Fisheries

TOMATO, CELERY AND SPRING ONION SALAD

Serves two

The secret is to chop everything superfine.

2 large ripe tomatoes
(de-seeded and skinned if you like)
2 sticks of celery – use a potato peeler to de-string it
6 spring onions
Salt & pepper
Juice of a lemon
Olive oil (same volume as lemon juice)
Basil is an optional but very nice extra.

Sharpen your knife and chop all the ingredients into a very fine dice. Mix up a dressing of oil and lemon, pour over and season.

Nice straightaway or refrigerate for the next day.

Lovely with new boiled potatoes and any grilled or pan-fried fish.

OVEN BAKED POTATO WEDGES

Easy-to-make and a million times better than the frozen type.

Cut medium size potatoes in half and par-boil for 8 minutes.

When cool enough to handle cut them into fat wedges.

Put 2 tablespoons of good olive oil in a bowl with salt and good grinding of black pepper (or try smoked paprika for a change) Tip the potatoes in and mix them round until completely coated.

Heat the oven to 200°C(Gas 6). Arrange the potato wedges thin side up on a shallow oven tray and bake for half an hour or until they are golden.

These are amazing with aioli (garlic mayonnaise) and any grilled or pan-fried fish.

For a change try sprinkling a few sprigs of Rosemary amongst the potatoes while they are cooking.

samphire

SALT-BAKED BLACK BREAM

1 large
BLACK BREAM
(about 800g)
2 lemons or limes
Small bunch parsley
1 bulb fennel
2kg sea salt

Clean and scale the fish but leave whole. Stuff the fish with chopped parsley, chopped fennel and slices of lemon or lime.

Cover the bottom of a deepish dish with sea salt to the depth of about 3cm.

Place the fish on the salt and cover with another 3.5cm of salt.

Wet the salt well with water and pat down gently so that a good crust forms over the fish as it cooks.

Place in a hot oven (220°C or Gas 7) for 15 - 20 minutes for the given weight – adjust the timing depending on the size and thickness of the fish.

When done let the fish cool a little and then gently remove the fish from the dish and break away all the salt and remove the skin.

Jan Baldwin
Winchelsea Beach.

Serve with home made mayonnaise and lemon or lime wedges.

fennel

BASQUE FISH STEW (MARMITAKO)

Serves 4
1.5 kg of white fish fillets try MONKFISH, COD or COLEY
4 tbsp olive oil
1 Onion chopped
6 garlic cloves
2 teaspoons paprika
¼ teaspoon of salt
¼ teaspoon of pepper
Small red chilli
6 tomatoes (or one can of chopped tomatoes)
1 kg potatoes
1 glass dry white wine
Half a cup of water

Diana J Holubowicz
St Leonards on Sea

Cut the fish into 3cm chunks.
Heat the oil in a heatproof casserole and saute the chopped onions, garlic and peppers, cleaned of seeds and cut into strips. When they are soft, add the tomatoes, peeled, seeded and chopped, the paprika, salt and pepper and chilli. When tomatoes are somewhat reduced add the potatoes, cut in dice.
Stir for a few minutes, then add the wine and water.
Cover the pot and cook on a high heat until the potatoes are nearly tender (about 20 minutes).
Add the fish to the casserole, cover and cook another 6 minutes or until fish flakes easily but is still juicy.
Take off heat for 15 minutes and let rest.
Reheat till casserole starts to bubble and remove from heat once again to sit for 5-10 minutes before serving.

CHILLI MACKEREL FOR TWO

2 whole MACKEREL (gutted with gills and heads removed)
4 fresh bay leaves
4 slices of lemon
Olive oil
Sea salt
Good pinch of dried chilli flakes
Watercress to garnish

Sharon Bartlett
Hastings Old Town

Place the fish in an ovenproof dish
Tuck 2 bay leaves and 2 lemon slices in each fish
Pour dessert spoonful of olive oil over each fish and season well with sea salt.
Bake in a hot oven (220°C or Gas 7) for 20 minutes.
Remove and scatter with the dried chilli flakes.
Bake for a further 5 minutes until the skins are blistered.
Garnish with watercress.
Serve with new potatoes, lemon-glazed carrots and courgettes sautéed with garlic.

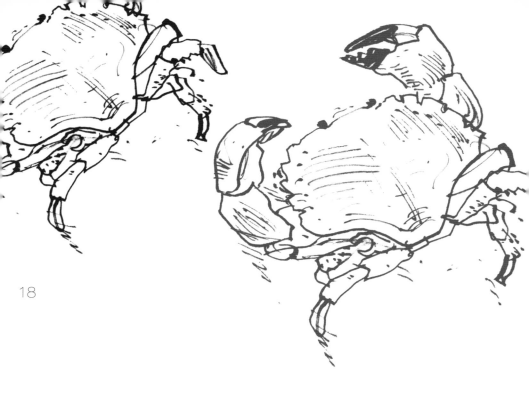

Cookery writer and photographer **ALASTAIR HENDY** has a house in Hastings Old Town and is a big fan of our delicious local crabs. He has donated these two recipes – one perfect for a party and the other a scrumptious quick snack.

CRAB QUICHE

1 x 375g packet
ready-made
shortcrust pastry
40g butter
5 small shallots,
finely chopped
6 large eggs
300ml sour cream
300ml double cream
Pinch saffron stamens,
warmed in 1 tbsp milk
Salt and black pepper

Serves 8 - 10

Crab and egg heaven. A cress or water-cress salad bound with a Dijon mustard vinaigrette makes matters perfect on serving. Eat on the day of making – refrigeration does it no favours.
Lightly grease and base line a 23 cm diameter x 5 cm deep loose-bottomed metal tart tin.Roll out the pastry to a £1 coin thickness and use to line the tin, leaving the edges overhanging. Prick the base and bake blind in a

**A good grating
nutmeg or
½ tsp ground mace
2 large
DRESSED CRABS,
brown meat separated
from white
Mustard cress or
watercress, to serve**

180°C oven (Gas 4) for 15 minutes.
Trim off the overhang.
Gently fry shallots in the butter until
translucent but not browned.
Beat the eggs with the creams, saffron
milk, salt and pepper, then fold in the
cooked shallot and white crab meat.
Mash the nutmeg into the brown meat
and then spread this
across the base of the pre-baked pastry
case. Spoon the crab and egg
mixture on top.
Bake in a 190C oven for 40 minutes,
or until risen a little
and pale golden brown on top.

**1 DRESSED CRAB
2 tbsp mayonnaise
1 tbsp chopped chives
(or green part of
spring onion)
½ long mild red chilli,
finely chopped
1 lemon - ½ juiced,
2 quarters to serve
Sea salt and
black pepper
Handful coriander
leaves (thoroughly
rinsed and drained)
Sourdough bread,
toasted/grilled and
rubbed with olive oil
Rocket and watercress,
tossed with Dijon
mustard dressing**

Alastair Hendy

CRAB TOAST WITH CHILLI AND LEMON MAYONNAISE

Spread brown meat on to toast first
(mix with a drop of the mayo if not
spreadable).
Mix mayonnaise with white meat,
along with chilli, lemon juice
and chives.
Pile on to prepared toast, lightly season
and pile loads of coriander on top.

CRUSTED GURNARD FILLETS

Serves 4 greedy people
6 GURNARDS filleted,
3 fillets per person.
125g soft breadcrumbs
2tbsp chopped parsley
3-4 dried chillies,
crumbled
Black pepper and salt
Olive oil and butter

Jilly Sillem

Put all the dry ingredients in a large roomy bowl.
Rub the fillets in a little olive oil and coat with crumb mixture.
Shallow fry in a mixture of olive oil and butter.
Serve with crusty bread and salad or whatever takes your fancy.

THE FILO FISH CAKES

The First In Last Out Pub in the Old Town High Street is famous for brewing its own beer, a roaring winter fire, free music nights and tasty wholesome meals cooked by Sharon Bigg.

makes approx 20
1.5kg
MIX OF SUSTAINABLE
LOCAL FISH
(depending on
time of year)
Filleted and skinned
450g potatoes
6 eggs
450g (approx) fresh
breadcrumbs
Salt & pepper
Plain flour
50g butter
150ml cream

Sharon Bigg

In large pan of salted simmering water, poach fish until just cooked, starting with the largest, thickest pieces. Should take between 4-8 mins.
Remove and leave to cool.
Peel and rough chop potatoes and boil in the same water.
Drain and mash with butter and cream, salt & pepper. Leave to cool.
Pick over fish removing all bones, skin etc. if not already done.
Place remaining fish in bowl and add mashed potato. Leave to cool
Place flour, beaten eggs and breadcrumbs on three separate plates.
Mould fish & potato mixture into balls.
Roll each ball in flour, then egg then breadcrumbs.
Flatten each into cake shape.
Shallow fry in oil until golden.

DOVER SOLE

Hastings is the only **DOVER SOLE** fishery in the world that has Marine Stewardship Council certification, so you know when you buy one that it has been caught using the most ethical and environmentally friendly methods.
This fish has a delicious and distinctive flavour and a firm, meaty texture, keep it simple, it doesn't need fancy 'restaurant' sauces to be fabulous.

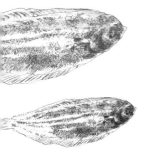

SONNY OF ROCK-A-NORE FISHERIES

says it is his favourite fish.
And he has a lot to choose from!
This is how he likes them -
"A small DOVER SOLE (called a slip) skinned and headed.
Flour and fry.
Just like mother used to do."

GRILLED DOVER SOLE

Skinned and filleted DOVER SOLE Melted butter Seasoning.

A simple, healthy and delicious luxury meal. Serve with new potatoes, peas or a crisp green salad. Brush the fillets with melted butter and season them with salt and black pepper.
Hot grill for 2-3 minutes each side.
That's it.

A SOLEFUL PAGE...

LEMON SOLE

Makes a good substitute if the budget won't stretch to dover sole. Try wrapping a whole fish in foil with butter, garlic and parsley and baking in the oven at 200°C(Gas 6) for 10-15mins depending on the size.

FAVOURITE FISH PIE

My step-father Douglas adored Hastings and would drive down on Friday gleefully anticipating good food and lively company. This was one of his one of his absolute favourites. Rock-a-nore Fisheries do a pie mix containing a very tasty mixture of their own smoked fish, salmon and white fish all chopped up and ready to go.

Serves 6
750g FISH PIE MIX
from Rock-a-Nore (or
your own selection)
2 eggs hardboiled
A bay leaf
Half litre milk plus
a bit extra for the
mashed potatoes
Knob of butter
1 heaped
tablespoon of flour
Seasoning
450g peeled floury
potatoes
(not waxy ones)
1 egg separated

Variation:
MAIKA CRAMPTON
sent in her mum's fish pie recipe which uses a similar combination of white fish and béchamel but also includes blanched carrots and dill. Her finishing touch is a buttered layering of scrunched up filo pastry sprinkled with cheese.

Chop the potatoes into quarters and put them on to boil.
Heat the milk and infuse the bay leaf.
Melt the butter in a pan, stir in the flour and cook and stir for at least 5 mins.
Add most of the milk, stirring all the time with a whisk to get rid of any lumps. When you have a smooth sauce the consistency of double cream – remove from the heat.
Arrange the fish in an ovenproof dish – check that every serving has a variety of flavours.
Cut the boiled eggs into quarters - wet a fine bladed knife to stop the egg sticking to it (a Tom Aikens tip!). Arrange them amongst the fish pieces.
Pour the sauce over the mixture and leave to cool a bit.
Meanwhile drain and mash the cooked potatoes with warm milk, butter, an egg yolk and seasoning. Whisk the white till dry and stiff then fold it into the potato. Spread this over the fish mixture and dot the top with butter.
Bake for 25-30 mins at 180°C.
The top will have risen and browned in peaks.
Serve with a rocket salad, samphire or another green seasonal vegetable.

FISH STEW WITH A SPANISH TWIST!

Large pinch saffron
Olive oil
Large onion
2 cloves garlic chopped
2 bay leaves
2 tbsp thyme
1 tsp sweet paprika
2 tins chopped tomato
250ml fish or veg stock
140g ground almonds
600g COD/HAKE/ HADDOCK (or any firm flesh white fish)– skinned, filleted and cut into 5cm chunks
12–16 raw prawns
12-16 mussels
12-16 clams
Grated orange peel (optional)
Garlic mayonnaise (optional)

Pam Smith
Hastings Old Town

Put saffron threads in an egg cup of boiling water and set aside to infuse.
Sauté onions in olive oil.
Add garlic, thyme, bay leaves.
Stir for a bit.
Add tomatoes, paprika and simmer for 5 mins
Stir in stock and saffron water
Add the ground almonds, bring to the boil stirring lots
Cook for 5 mins – it will thicken.
Gently stir in the white fish, prawns, mussels and clams.
Cover and simmer for 5 mins until fish and seafood cooked.
Stir in grated orange (optional).
Serve with crusty bread or roasted baby potatoes and a big blob of garlic mayonnaise.

Emerald Turner makes a similar fish stew and serves hers on slices of garlic-buttered ciabatta toast. **YUM!**

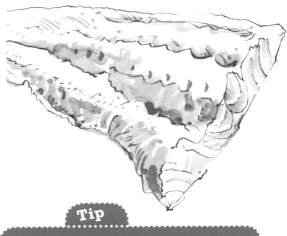

Tip
Try marinating raw fish as it's very healthy, quick and easy to prepare. *Tom Aikens*

FISHERMAN'S BALLS
(Bolinhas de bacalhau)

450g Local Hastings SALT COD
2 cups of mashed potato
2 tbsp of finely chopped parsley
2 large eggs
1 small onion
1 bay leaf
4 peppercorns
Salt and pepper, to taste
Fresh oil for frying

Soak the salt cod overnight and during the following morning, change water 3 times. Drain, remove skin and any bones, cut into chunks and put to one side.

In a pan simmer a small onion thinly sliced with a bay leaf and 4 peppercorns in 2 cups of water.

After 5 minutes, add the cod and 2 extra cups of water. When water starts to simmer again, cover pan and remove from heat.

To form the bolinhas (balls): drain the fish and flake it well into a bowl. Add the potatoes and the eggs beaten with a pinch of salt along with the parsley. Salt and pepper to taste.

Using your hands, form small balls and fry in fresh oil until golden brown.

Serve with some very cold beer or wine. Delicious!!

Samara Streeten
Hastings Old Town

24

SMOKED (AT ROCK-A-NORE) HADDOCK
with poached egg, mash, broad beans and pancetta

Serves 2
2 big fillets of
SMOKED HADDOCK
2 poached eggs
4 nice big
mashing potatoes
400g broad beans
100g pancetta cubes
Olive oil
Butter
Milk
salt, pepper
2 lemon quarters

This is my regular nights-are-drawing-in autumnal supper default... I always have the ingredients to hand, even if they're in the freezer (but it's lovelier if they're fresh, obviously). As well as being extremely cosy, comforting and genuinely heart-warming, it's also a complete doddle – 30 mins from start to finish — and is best consumed with a funky glass of white and the prospect of an evening in front of mindless Saturday night telly...

Bake the haddock, which has been dotted with a tiny knoblet of butter and crowned with a lemon quarter, wrapped in greased foil (oil if you're feeling worthy, butter if you're naughty) in the middle of the oven at 190 for 20-25 mins, depending on the size of your fillet. Meanwhile, boil your potatoes and mash in your preferred way with both butter and a few splashes of milk, so it really is super-creamy and you can make meringue-style peaks. While the broad beans are being either steamed or boiled, pan-fry your pancetta cubes for a couple of minutes on a hot flame, before stirring them into the cooked beans.

Make a bed of mash on the plate, serve the haddock on top of it and the beans and pancetta to one side, and make sure to poach your egg so that it really is ready at the very last minute- it'll take about five minutes so do it while the beans are cooking.

To serve, place your egg on top of your haddock, ensuring it is firm but still runny. The simple loveliness of this dish is the yellow-on-yellow-on-yellow, as the egg yolk is pierced, oozes over the smoked fish and into the mash. I have never served this to anything other than an accompaniment of gratifying 'mmmm!'s — with fish dishes the simple ones are invariably the crowd pleasers.

Kathryn Flett
Random-on-Sea

FILETS DE GURNARD
à la Judges

Serves 2
As many fillets
per person that
looks enough
(GURNARDS vary
wildly in size).
Judges bread-
crumbs (mixed
loaf styles adds to
the interest).
Olive oil.
A lemon.
Capers, if you like
them, about
a tablespoon.

Gurnard is the ugliest fish with the sweetest taste, but the supply of this splendid critter is quite variable, so you can make this with pretty much any other non-oily fish fillet. I developed this recipe as I have freezer full of breadcrumbs from leftover Judges bread I can't bear to waste..

Heat oven to 180°C (160°C if fan). Place the fillets in a ceramic baking dish, you have pre-drizzled with olive oil and drizzle a bit more over the fish. Mix a couple of handfuls of breadcrumbs with the zest of half the lemon. Pack it over the top of the fillets, pressing it on to a thickness of about half a centimetre. Squeeze the juice of the lemon over the top, so that the breadcrumbs stick together.

If you like capers, press them into the crust now. You can also add chopped parsley. Sprinkle over pepper and sea salt and bake in the oven.

Have a look after 10 minutes, poking with a sharp knife to see if the fish is cooked through. If it isn't give it another 5 minutes.

Maggie Alderson
Hastings Old Town

I usually serve this with brown basmati rice and green beans.

Tip

Almost any white fish is delicious if marinated in soy sauce, ginger and garlic-then either pan fried grilled or baked! **Caroline Burstein**

HELL'S KITCHEN PASTA

MUSSELS preferrably the smaller ones, about two dozen, as some inevitably will have to be discarded when they don't open up after steaming Olive Oil Small knob of butter Dry white wine Lemon juice Medium onion, chopped into small pieces Couple cloves of garlic Fresh coriander Coarse sea salt And of course, enough tagliatelle for two more)

*John Cole
Hastings*

This dish owes a huge debt to Marcella Hazan's The Classic Italian Cookbook and Craig Claiborne's The New York Times Cookbook. These two books were my Bibles of cooking when I lived in Hell's Kitchen, a district of New York City, some 25 years ago. Fresh pasta is essential to this recipe, so find a market or deli that sells it - or make it yourself!

Steam the mussels until they open. Chuck the ones that refuse to open up. Strain them, retaining a small cup of the water. Pull the meat from the shells, and then rinse the mussels in a colander to get rid of any residual grit.

Boil a big pot of water for the pasta, adding a splash of olive oil to help keep the pasta from sticking together.

In a large frying pan, gently fry the onion and garlic in olive oil and a small knob of butter until translucent yellow. Add the mussels and cook gently. When it all begins to bubble, add a splash of white wine and a couple of drops of lemon juice to taste. Let simmer gently for about five minutes, then turn down the heat, throw in a pinch of the coriander and sea salt. Cover and keep on the lowest heat possible. If the sauce begins to thicken too much, add a bit of the left over mussel water.

As the pasta water comes to a rolling boil, prepare warmed pasta bowls. Fresh pasta takes minutes to cook. The pasta will continue to cook after its been served, so taste test and drain the pasta while still its al dente.

Heap pasta into warmed bowls and then ladle the mussel sauce on top.

Add a pinch of coarse sea salt and finely chopped coriander and you're there. Enjoy!

27

MUSSELS
Eat mussels when there is an R in the month. To clean: Soak in a bowl of water. Use the back of a knife to scrape off any barnacles and the beards. Tap them and throw out any that do not close.

HUSS SALTIMBOCCA

Serves 4
800g – 1kg HUSS
12 thin slices
pancetta
Small bunch sage
Olive oil
6 ripe tomatoes
skinned & de-seeded
1 large onion
halved & sliced
75g sugar
½ cup balsamic or
sherry vinegar

1. Pre-heat the oven to 220°C
2. Cut the huss into 4 equal pieces.
3. With a sharp knife cut right along the top of the fish down to the bone.
4. Put 2 or 3 sage leaves in each piece then season the fish (not too heavy on the salt as pancetta is quite salty).
5. Wrap the pancetta around the fish and set aside in the fridge.

The confit
1. To skin tomatoes, make a cross on top and bottom & plunge into boiling water. When the skin starts to peel, remove and peel off all the skin. Cut into quarters, scoop out the seeds and discard. Chop the flesh and set aside.
2. Sweat the onion in some olive oil.
3. Add the tomato and cook for a few more minutes until the tomato starts to break down.
4. Add 75g sugar, ½ cup balsamic or sherry vinegar.
5. Cook it down until it thickens and looks like a chutney.
6. Add a few finely chopped sage leaves at the end of cooking.

The Huss
1. Heat some oil in a pan. It wants to be hot but not smoking.
2. Put the huss pieces in, and turn until the pancetta is browned.
3. Transfer to a hot over dish and bake in the oven for approx 15-20 mins or until the fish comes away from the bone (to test, put a fork next to the bone).
4. Serve with some of the confit, new potatoes and buttered spinach.

POMEGRANATE
Food & Drink House
Hastings Old Town

JAMAICAN MACKEREL

Serves 4
450-500g MACKEREL
6 green bananas OR
use potatoes
2-3 tbsp vegetable oil
2 onions, sliced
2 tomatoes, chopped
2 spring onions,
chopped
Scotch bonnet or chilli
pepper to taste,
finely chopped
Juice of two limes

Elspeth Thompson
Winchelsea Beach

Soak the mackerel overnight in water with 1 tsp lime juice added.

Peel green bananas (or potatoes if using instead) and boil in unsalted water for 10 mins. Drain and set in bottom of a large oven-proof dish (slice potatoes thickly; bananas can be left whole).

Heat the oil in a saucepan. Saute the onions and spring onions till translucent and add the tomatoes and hot peppers – start with one small one, finely chopped. Cook for 5 mins or so to make a sauce.

Lay the mackerel, whole or in thick slices, on top of the green bananas. Pour over the tomato and pepper sauce and bake in medium oven for 30-40 minutes.

skate wing

JANE'S SKATE
WITH CAPER SAUCE

2 small wings of
SKATE (200-250g)
(Note that skate is
endangered and most of
what is sold as skate is
now Ray
1 tbsp seasoned flour
2 tablespoons
sunflower oil
4 anchovy fillets
drained and chopped
1 tbsp capers drained
2 tablespoons
chopped parsley
2 tbsp sherry vinegar
Juice of half a lemon
Small piece of butter
Ground black pepper

Jane Scruton
Hastings Old Town

This is a classic way to cook skate.
Use kitchen scissors to trim the frilly
edge from the wings, dry them on
kitchen paper and dredge with the
seasoned flour.
Heat a non-stick pan and add the oil.
When the oil starts to smoke - add the
wings. Fry them until the flesh looks
creamy white. Keep them warm on a
serving plate.
Using the same hot pan first add the
sherry vinegar which will bubble and
spit then the butter, lemon juice,
anchovies, capers and pepper.
Finally sprinkle on the parsley, heat
through and pour over the wings.

31

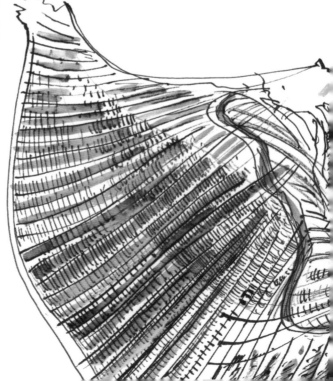

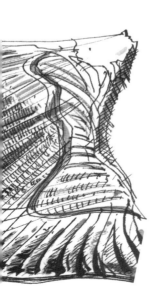

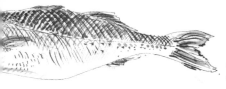

JAPANESE STYLE MACKEREL

Serves 4
4 small local
MACKEREL, head and
tails trimmed off
Marinade:
4 tbsp mirin sauce
(available from
Judges)
3 tbsp Soy sauce
1 tbsp sake
Pepper and salt
Salad:
Small cucumber
2 sticks celery
Small head of fennel
Handful of samphire
(if in season)
3 large spring onions
4 tbsp rice Wine
(or cider) vinegar
Handful of fresh mint

Mackerel marinated with mirin, soy sauce and sake and served with a crunchy, lightly pickled salad. Thai fragrant rice makes a good accompaniment.

Method:
1. Mix together marinade ingredients in a shallow dish.
2. Slash mackerel diagonally along either side.
3. Marinade mackerel for an hour, turning the fish every 15 minutes.
4. Prepare the salad while the fish is marinating – finely chop the cucumber, celery, fennel and spring onions.
5. Carefully wash samphire, blanch it briefly in boiling water and then plunge it in cold water and drain. Add to other ingredients.
6. Chop mint finely, place in small bowl and pour over 3 tbsp boiling water.
7. Add vinegar to mint and water and season well with salt and pepper.
8. Add vinegar mixture to salad ingredients. Chill it in fridge until needed.
9. Heat grill.
10. Transfer mackerel with marinade into a heatproof dish and grill for approximately 4 minutes, turn over and grill for another 4 minutes.
11. Serve on a bed of rice and spoon the remaining marinade over the fish and the rice.
12. Serve the salad alongside.

Stephanie Donaldson
Hastings Old Town

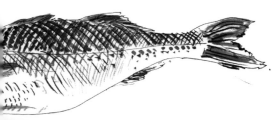

SEAFOOD TEMPURA (Japanese style)

250ml iced fizzy water
150g SR white flour
WHITE FISH, SQUID,
PRAWNS
button mushrooms
red peppers
French beans,
asparagus
batons of carrot
batons of courgette

This is a great dish to serve for friends, in much the same way as a fondue used to be back in the day.

It is full of excitement and drama as the selected pieces are dipped in the icy batter then dropped into hot oil where they puff up and float to the top, taking seconds to cook to a crisp.

Drain the cooked pieces on kitchen paper and serve them immediately with a salty dipping sauce.

Vary the flavours and textures and it will be a truly memorable meal.

Prepare the raw ingredients by cutting everything to more or less the same size and arrange in pretty colourful piles ready to go.

Whisk the batter ingredients together very lightly and use it straight away. Lumpy batter for tempura is fine.

* You can now buy
Tempura Batter
Mixture that is
quite foolproof!

Dip in the batter and fry in hot oil in batches and drain the pieces on kitchen paper, then serve and eat while one of you continues frying.

We tend to do one flavour at a time, alternating a fish with a vegetable until we cannot eat another scrap!

Serve with a soy dipping sauce.
This can be straight from the bottle, but it's even better if you prepare your own. Take 1 finely grated cube of fresh ginger, 1 crushed clove of garlic, finely chopped half red chilli, one dessertspoonful of sugar, 2 tbsp of rice wine or lemon juice and 3 tbsp of soy sauce. Put all these together and heat to a simmer then set aside to cool.

LOBSTER HOT DOGS

**Order a
FRESH LOBSTER
to be cooked and
collected from
Rock-a-Nore.
2 tbsp good
Mayonaisse
Cayenne pepper or
Tabasco sauce
2 sticks of celery
Squeeze of lemon
Best bread rolls**

Hot dogs are such cheap fast-food that to mention Lobster in the same breath seems ridiculous - but bear with me! I owe a big debt of gratitude to Maggie Alderson, who, on noticing my food obsession, gave me a copy of Jeffrey Steingarten's book The Man Who Ate Everything. This is where I discovered the Lobster hot dog that residents of Maine USA are all too familiar with. Hastings isn't exactly Maine but we do catch lobsters here. This makes an expensive but unforgettable snack.

Break the shell with special instruments or use pliers and a hammer to extract all the meat from the tail, legs and claws. (Don't waste the shell. Crush it and boil up in water to make a great stock base.) In a mixing bowl for each cup of lobster meat add:

2 tbsp of good mayonnaise;

A stalk or two of finely chopped celery (this is where the crunch comes from – not from bits of shell!).

A pinch or two of cayenne or a dash of Tabasco, a squeeze of lemon and seasoning.

Mix up being careful not to break up the lobster meat – you want a few nice chunks.

VITAL: Use very good soft rolls (Judges Bakery's are recommended!). Split and toast under the grill till golden inside. I can't stress the importance of toasting enough. It seals the bread surface and stops it becoming soggy.

Assemble & Devour.

MACKEREL A LA MAROCAINE

Multiply ingredients
by number of fish
1 MACKEREL, cleaned
Juice of 1/2 lemon
1 heaped tsp
cumin powder
1/4 tsp salt

CRAIG SAMS
a wise man of food
Hastings Old Town

So simple to make, use freshly caught mackerel and you can't go wrong. Bake mackerel at 180°C(Gas 4) for 20 minutes or until well done.
Allow to cool down and dry out.
Then carefully remove the flesh from the bones.
Add the lemon juice, cumin and salt and mix thoroughly, flaking the mackerel and incorporating the seasonings throughout the mixture.
Adjust seasonings to taste.
Serve with couscous or rice.

35

VAGUELY ORIENTAL FISH & UDON NOODLES

Serves 4.
BROTH
1.5l boiling water
2-3 cloves of garlic
1-2 red chillies
de-seeded and
finely chopped
Root ginger - a
conker-sized piece,
peeled and chopped
125ml soy sauce
1 bunch spring onions,
chopped including
green stems

FISH
500g WHITE FISH
(MONKFISH or
POLLACK) in large
chunks raw prawns if
you're feeling rich

NOODLES & VEG
4 servings of brown
rice udon noodles
(3 servings per packet)
Any or all of
the following:
Sliced mushrooms,
Sliced courgettes,
peeled and diced
Butternut squash,
Pak choy or sea kale,
Thinly sliced carrots.

GARNISH
Half a lime per
person and handful of
chopped coriander

Inspired by lovely meals eaten at Viet Hoa in Kingsland Road and Wagamama.

Make broth by simmering first six ingredients for a minute or two. Taste and add more soy sauce if necessary.
Add noodles and veg, stir and simmer for 3 minutes.
Add fish. Lay them on top and cover and simmer for 3 minutes or until fish is white through and prawns opaque and pink.
Serve in large bowls with juice of half a lime and a handful or coriander on top with extra soy sauce on the side.

Lesley Greening Lassoff

MEDITERRANEAN SQUID
WITH PRAWNS AND BROAD BEANS

Serves 4
500g whole cleaned
SQUID or CUTTLEFISH
250g fresh, shelled
PRAWNS
2 tbsp extra virgin
olive oil
2 garlic cloves,
finely sliced
250g shelled
broad beans
1 glass dry sherry
1 glass water
1 tsp fresh, chopped
marjoram or oregano
Salt & pepper

The true taste of the Mediterranean is right here on our doorstep with this flavour-packed recipe made from one of the best fish to be found all year in our local waters – the humble squid. Unlike some squid dishes where it's all about flash-frying and serving up instantly, key to this dish is slow, gentle cooking to let the squid release its juices and infuse with the rich flavour of the beans.

Heat the oil gently in a large frying pan or wok. Add the garlic and let it soften then swiftly add the squid and let it cook gently in its own juices for around ten minutes. Then add the beans, the sherry and the water and bring it to the boil before sprinkling in the seasoning and herbs. Once it's bubbling gently, turn down the heat so it's just simmering, add a lid and leave it to conjure up its magic for around 20 mins, or until the fish is tender.

Once it's nearly done remove the lid, test your seasoning and add the prawns. Turn up the heat to evaporate some of the juices and the prawns will cook almost instantly. Don't leave it too long otherwise they'll get floury and rather chewy. Serve with a fresh green salad and some chunky organic bread to mop up the juices. *Mediterranean bliss!*

Alastair Fairley
Hastings Old Town

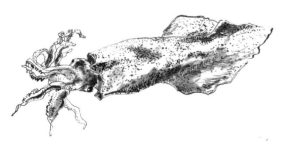

FRESH COCKLES WITH PASTA

Serves 2-4
Half a pint of
FRESH COCKLES
(not in vinegar)
2 good sized
Knobs of butter
Handful of fresh
chopped parsley
Half a glass of
white wine
2 shallots,
chopped fine.
Packet of Fine
spaghetti or linguini,
servings for 2 or 4
Splash of olive oil

Put a large pan of salted water on to boil and add the pasta.
Melt the butter in a pan and add the shallots – cook gently till transparent then add the wine, turning up the heat for a minute or two and stirring as it reduces.
Reduce the heat, add the cockles and chopped parsley and warm through for one minute then remove from the heat.
Drain the pasta then pour it back into the pan with a splash of olive oil.
Stir in the shallots, parsley and cockles.
Serve immediately with a nice chilled glass of white wine.

Half a pint of
FRESH COCKLES
smokey bacon
bread for toast

Variation: **WITH BACON ON TOAST.**

Add thin strips of smoky bacon at the shallot-frying stage, then proceed as above.
Pile the mixture onto slices of buttered toast.

> **Tip**
>
> My favourite seafood to eat in the summer is grilled hand-dived scallops in their shell, drizzled with olive oil, garlic and rosemary, finished with a little lemon juice on the BBQ   *Tom Aikens*

POTTED CRAB

25g butter
1 dressed crab
(about100g
crab meat
white and
brown)
Half tsp
nutmeg
Half tsp
cayenne pepper
Salt and pepper
Juice of
one lemon
Few sprigs
of parsley,
chopped

Melt the butter in a thick-based
saucepan, being careful not to burn.
Stir in the crab meat and seasonings and
cook gently till all the crab is coated
in butter.
Remove from heat, stir in lemon juice and
chopped parsley and spoon into small
bowls or ramekins. Serve warm on toast.

Elspeth Thompson

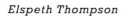

MARINATED MOUNT'S BAY SARDINES
with olive oil, lemon & oregano

Serves 4
8 SARDINES
3 tbsp Greek olive oil
1 tbsp lemon juice
Lamb's lettuce
Vine ripened
cherry tomatoes
Oregano

Rick Stein
The Seafood Restaurant

Fillet sardines, gently removing skin but leaving membrane behind. Season with salt and pepper, add lemon juice and olive oil and leave for 20 minutes. Cut cherry tomatoes in half and mix together with the lamb's lettuce. To serve place lettuce and tomatoes on plate with sardines on top. Season as required and sprinkle lightly with oregano.

41

CUTTLEFISH TAPAS
(Sepia Officinalis)

Cuttlefish fishing is a messy business; you know when they're cuttling locally, as the boat's tractors are covered in sepia black ink.
The inks,secreted in self defence are intended for the cuttlefish's predators. But it also has a delicious favour and, added to a tomato sauce, makes the perfect vehicle to braise the cuttlefish and form a pasta sauce.
It was a lovely surprise to find cuttlefish being landed in Hastings. It's is a great favourite of mine and the first thing I'll order on a foreign holiday. Cuttlefish, squid and octopus are collectively known as cephalopods, they aren't everybody's cup of tea but this dish hasn't budged in four years on our menu at St Clement's.
If you can find very small cuttlefish then don't worry about blanching them - go straight to stage 2.

STAGE 1
2 large CUTTLEFISH
1 healthy shot of
white wine vinegar
1 large pinch of sea salt
1 bay leaf

Clean as you would a squid and discard all the innards. Place in a saucepan with salt, vinegar and bay leaf, add some water but do not fully cover the fish. Bring to boil, cover with a lid and turn to a simmer and cook for 20 minutes. The fish will exude some liquid and stew in its own stock. Leave to cool for a couple of hours, drain, discard liquor and remove any skin, and tough bits.
Cut the fish into match size pieces ready for frying.

STAGE 2
Cooked and cleaned
CUTTLEFISH
Extra virgin olive oil
Smoked Paprika
Chopped wild garlic
or garlic
Sherry vinegar (push
the boat out and get the
best you can find you
only need a splash)
Sliced cooked waxy
new potatoes,
Charlottes are good.
Chopped parsley
Small capers
Maldon sea salt

Nick Hales
Chef/Patron
at St Clements Restaurant
St Leonards on Sea

Heat a frying pan, add the olive oil, add the potatoes and start to crisp. Once they have a little colour add the cuttlefish, cook for a minute then add chopped garlic. Once the garlic is golden brown add a slug of sherry vinegar and the paprika and a bit more olive oil to form a dressing.

Add capers, sea salt to taste and herbs and serve with plenty of crispy bread to mop up juices.

A perfect tapas style dish.

43

st. Clement's

FAVOURITE FRIDAY FISH DISH

**2 white fish cutlets –
we used COD in those
days but *POLLACK* or
COLEY are fine
100g grated
Cheddar cheese
Knob of butter
Finely chopped onion
Salt and pepper**

**Maureen Charlesworth served
four terms as Mayor of Hastings**
and works tirelessly to promote the town
and its residents. She sent us this recipe
from the days when she ran a small hotel
with her late husband. It was always
popular with their guests.

Fry the onion gently till transparent
and soft.
Mix it with the grated cheese.
Season it with salt and pepper.
Part-cook the fish cutlets under the grill.
Spread this mixture on top of the
cutlets and put them back under the
grill, until the cheese is all nicely melted
over the fish.

Maureen Charlesworth

44

PLAICE
WITH QUICK CUCUMBER SAUCE

750g PLAICE fillets
75g butter or
margarine
2 x 15 ml spoons of
anchovy paste or
3 x 15 ml spoons of
anchovy essence
1 small cucumber,
diced
1 tsp chopped
fresh dill
One 300ml
can of condensed
mushroom soup
4 x 15 ml spoons of
plain yoghurt
1 tomato, skinned,
seeded and chopped
Salt
Freshly ground
black pepper

Michael Foster

**Michael Foster MP for Hastings
& Rye for 13 years** is a keen cook
and this is one of his favourite recipes.

I just love local plaice. And grilled
plaice with a quick cucumber sauce
brings out all the flavours. The dish will
take about 15 minutes to prepare and the
cooking time is around 15 minutes.
I prefer the plaice skin to be removed
but that is not necessary; it's a matter
of taste.

45

How to do it:
Rinse the fillets and dry them well.
Melt the butter in a frying pan then add
the anchovy paste or essence and the
fillets.
Fry over a medium heat until the fish is
golden, turning just once.
In a bowl combine the remaining ingredients, adding salt and pepper to taste,
and spoon over the fish.
Cover the pan and heat through gently
for about 5 minutes.
Remove the fillets to a warm serving dish
and pour over the sauce.
Enjoy!

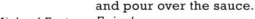

MY PLAICE

1 PLAICE fillet
1 tomato chopped fine.
Salad leaves, dressed
the way you like it
Butter/olive oil
Seasoned flour
Fresh bread

I love the look of food on a plate and colours are very important, so I find it very difficult to resist buying fresh Plaice fillets, they are just so pretty with their red spots. This is my perfect lunch for one.

Dust the fish with seasoned flour.
Heat the fat in a shallow frying pan.
Add the fish, skin side down.
Cook for 2 mins then turn it over and do the same on the other side.
Test with the point of a knife that the fish is milky white right through.
Drain the fish on kitchen paper and arrange everything on a nice plate.
To make this meal perfect eat it with a slice of Potato & Thyme Bread from the Lighthouse Bakery sold at Plenty in St Leonards.

POACHED LEMON SOLE FILLETS
WITH A WINE SAUCE

1-2 LEMON SOLE fillets per person depending on size, skin on
Small handful of thyme
3 bay leaves
Large handful of parsley
Stick of celery roughly chopped
Small handful of fennel or dill fronds
Thick slice of white onion
1 small carrot washed and roughly chopped
Glass of white wine
Juice of half a lemon plus a large strip of zest
1 tbsp of olive oil
50-70g of butter
Salt and black pepper

Lesley at Blackrock House - a most luxurious B&B in Central Hastings

Delicious fresh lemon sole or another flat fish is fine for this dish. A simple green salad is an ideal accompaniment or, for a true breath of the sea, a big handful of samphire washed and blanched for a couple of minutes in boiling water. Place the fillets in a largish flat pan with all the ingredients just immersed in water and put a lid on.

Bring the pan slowly to the boil and then turn down to simmer till tender. This will only take a few minutes. Check to ensure that fish does not overcook.

Once cooked through, place on a dish and cover to prevent from drying out, while you prepare the rest of the sauce.

Sauce

Strain the cooking liquor and then place back on a high heat to reduce and thicken. Add the butter towards the end of the process to enrich the sauce. Check for seasoning and add salt and pepper as needed. When the sauce has reached a suitable consistency for serving, pour it over the fish fillets.

Alternatively, skip the sauce and serve the fish with a good dollop of Aioli.

ROO'S SQUASH & MONKFISH CURRY

1 medium sized Butternut squash peeled and cubed
One MONKFISH TAIL cut into cubes – you could also use *LARGE PRAWNS* or *LOBSTER*

2 medium onions
1 large red chilli
A one inch cube of fresh ginger
2 large cloves of garlic.

SPICES
1 tsp Black peppercorns
1 tsp fenugreek
1 tsp salt
1–2 tsp cumin
1–2 tsp yellow mustard seeds
25 curry leaves (a good handful)

1 tin coconut milk
turmeric
1 large bunch or packet of spinach
Basmati rice
Popadums

Rupert Walton
St Leonards-on-Sea

In a blender: whizz up the onions, chilli, ginger, and garlic with a little water till you get a paste.

Toast the spices in a heavy iron pan for a few secs. *Don't let them burn.*

Add the blended onion mixture plus a tin of coconut milk, half a tsp of tumeric, half a glass of water and the cubed squash.

Simmer with the lid on for one hour or until the squash is tender.

Add spinach and monkfish

Stir and cook for 5 mins or until the fish turns milky white.

Serve with rice and popadums.

48

ROAST SEABASS
WITH SALSA VERDE MAYONNAISE

Serves 4
FOR THE FISH
1 SEABASS, 1.5-2kg,
scaled and gutted (or 2
smaller fish, between
750g and 1kg each)
Lemon
Fennel seeds
Olive oil
Maldon salt
FOR THE SALSA VERDE
mayonnaise
2 egg yolks
1 tsp Dijon
mustard
Salt and pepper
Up to 300ml light olive
oil (or a mix of a
neutral oil such as
sunflower or
groundnut and extra
virgin olive oil)
2 cloves of garlic,
peeled
6 anchovy fillets
(rinsed,
if packed in salt)
2 tbs capers, rinsed
Generous handful of
parsley leaves
Generous handful of
chervil leaves (or
fennel tops, or other
soft green herb such
as basil or mint)

Louise Bell
St Leonards on Sea

Preheat oven to 200°C. Put a few slices of lemon inside the fish, plus a generous sprinkling of fennel seeds. Season with Maldon salt, inside and out, place in a roasting dish and drizzle generously with olive oil. Roast for about 25 minutes (for a single large fish) or 15-20 minutes (for two smaller fish). Test for doneness – the fish is cooked when the flesh is opaque, but still moist, and easily comes away from the bone.

Meanwhile, make the mayonnaise. Beat together the egg yolks, mustard and salt and pepper. Then gradually whisk in the oil or oils, at first drop by drop then in a thin stream. If the mixture threatens to curdle, add an ice cube or splash of ice-cold water and whisk hard. Stop when it looks like the egg yolks can't take any more oil, and you have a thick mayonnaise mixture. Add a generous squeeze of lemon juice. Finely chop the garlic, anchovies, capers and herbs by hand or in a food processor, and add to the mayonnaise.

Serve the fish and mayonnaise together. Puy lentils or new potatoes would be nice.

Tip

The easiest way to cook fish for a picnic is by placing your fillets of fish on a tray, sprinkling with a little olive oil, seasoning, a little lemon zest, some fresh thyme and then placing under a hot grill for 3-4 minutes. *Tom Aikens*

SEA TROUT IN BEER

**1 SEA TROUT or other fresh local fish. (cleaned, gutted and scaled)
Can of beer/lager or stout
Fresh herbs - like Parsley, Lemon Thyme or Dill
2 cloves of Garlic
the local paper & string**

*Dave Watkins
St Leonards-on-Sea
– with a beery nod to
Jamie Oliver!*

It seems unlikely but wrapping a fish in newspaper then soaking it in beer before you bake it in the oven is actually a very good idea! *Try it.*

Stuff the fish with herbs and season inside.
Wrap it up well in newspaper and tie with string.
Soak the fish parcel in beer until it is all absorbed.
Bake in oven at 200°C(Gas 6) for 20 minutes.
Take off paper and the skin comes off with it.
Serve with new potatoes and greens.

51

Fillet of cod

Stocks ARE replenishing and one day, fish fingers crossed, locally landed cod may be back on the menu.

SEVICHE OR CEVICHE

2 skinned **SEA BASS** or
LEMON SOLE **fillets**
2 crushed
cloves of garlic
1 x red chilli finely
sliced in rounds
1 onion sliced
into fine rings
Juice of 2 limes
Pepper and salt

This is a very popular way of preparing fish in South America where fish is 'cooked' using the acidity of lime or lemon juice instead of heat.
We have to thank our friend Michael Blann (who travelled so much in South America that we now call him Miguel) to thank for introducing this to us.

Place onion rings in a glass dish and cover with the fish.
Cover the fish in lime juice.
Sprinkle with fine sliced chilli and crushed garlic.
Cover and refrigerate for 4 hours.
Serve with fresh crusty bread and salad.

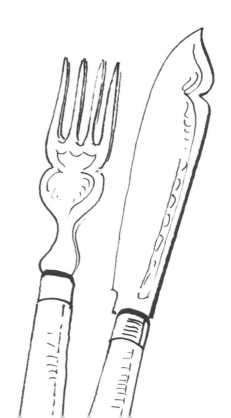

STEWART'S MUM'S BAKED FISH
WITH LEMON MASH

Serves 2
I x large or 2-3 small
fillets of WHITE FISH
(GURNARD/COLEY/
POLLACK OR
HADDOCK)
Sliced fresh tomatoes
Mushrooms -
(sliced if large)
Glass of white wine
Half a sliced lemon
Butter
Parsley
Salt and pepper

This is so easy and delicious.
Remove skin from fish and tweak out any remaining bones.
Lay mushrooms in bottom of baking dish and dot with butter.
Place fish on top of mushrooms, season and dot with butter.
Place sliced lemon on top of the fish.
Arrange slices of tomato on top of fish and lemon and pour a glass of white wine over the top.
Season with more black pepper and dot with butter.
Cook at 190°C for 25 mins.
Cover with foil and bake for 15 mins.
Remove foil and bake for another 10 mins.
Serve in bowls sprinkled with chopped parsley and mashed potato flavoured with grated lemon zest.

If you can't wait for mashed potato this is also nice with lots of crusty fresh bread.

QUICK KIPPER PATE

A pair of KIPPERS
25g butter
75g full-fat
cream cheese
The juice of a lemon
Half tsp horseradish
A pinch of paprika
Black pepper to taste.

Mark Storr-Hoggins

Poach the kippers in a pan of simmering water for 8 minutes.
Remove and allow to cool. Pick over the fish, removing all the skin and bones.
Put the fish in a food processor with the cream cheese, lemon juice, horseradish and paprika. Pulse to a coarse soft pâté.
Place in a suitable container, covered with clingfilm and chill until ready to eat on crusty bread or toast.

SMOKED HADDOCK CHOWDER

450g un-dyed
SMOKED HADDOCK
1lt milk
1 bay leaf
1 large baking potato
peeled and chopped
small
1 chopped onion
Knob of butter
Fresh parsley chopped

This makes a quick, warming treat
served with crusty fresh bread.
Fry the chopped onion in butter till soft
and translucent.
Add potato pieces and bayleaf and cook
for 5 mins.
Add the haddock and the milk and cook
for a further 10 minutes until the potato
is done. Take two cups of
the mixture and blend it briefly to give
the soup a thicker consistency, then
stir everything together and serve in
warmed bowls sprinkled with freshly
chopped parsley.

55

Another quick and tasty

SMOKED HADDOCK DISH

from DEX
at Rock-a-nore Fisheries
- where they smoke
their own.
"Serve smoked haddock
with crushed new
potatoes topped with
poached eggs and lots of
cracked black pepper."

SMOKED MACKEREL & RICE

**500g SMOKED
MACKEREL, flaked
and deboned
2 onions sliced and
chopped
2 tbsp oil
2 tbsp butter
2 large tomatoes
skinned and chopped
1 tsp chilli powder
Freshly ground
black pepper
2 cups cooked rice
5 tbsp sultanas
(optional)
Squeeze of lemon
chopped parsley**

Heat oil and butter in a saucepan and
saute onions until golden brown.
Add tomatoes, chilli and pepper, cook
for a little longer.
Add fish and rice and optional sultanas.
Cook over a low heat until
heated through.
Before serving stir in a squeeze of lemon
juice and sprinkle with chopped parsley.

*Lisa and Emmanuel
Judges Bakery
Hastings Old Town*

SPICEY FRIED FISH BITES

Great party food recipe from the
Old Town Deli mobile catering company

Serves 6

**1kg WHITE FISH cut
into thin strips
(use most plentiful
catch of the day)
Salt to taste
5 tsp lemon juice
2 tsp White pepper
2 tsp red chilli powder
or more ...
some like it hot !
2 tsp Turmeric
120g gram
(chickpea) flour
60g garlic Paste
60g ginger Paste
¼ cup of white vinegar
500ml vegetable oil
3 tsp chaat masala
(Indian spice mix)**

Method
1. Prick the fish with a sharp fork.
2. Rub salt and lemon juice over the fish
pieces and set aside for 1-2 hours.
3. Mix all the other ingredients in a bowl
except the chaat masala and oil.
4. Dip the fish pieces in the batter and let
them stand for another half an hour.
5. Heat the oil in a wok. Deep-fry
the fish pieces on medium heat.
6. Sprinkle the fish with chaat masala
and serve with sliced cucumbers,
tomatoes and lemon wedges.

57

SPIKE'S SUSTAINABLE SALADE NICOISE

To feed 4 as a main course with green salad
4-6 SMOKED MACKEREL fillets
4-6 hard boiled eggs
500g salad potatoes (Anya/Pink Fir Apple or similar)
200g green beans
1 tin anchovies in oil
2 tsp capers, chopped
3-4 tbsp good home- made dressing
Handful of chopped fresh herbs (parsley, mint, basil)
1/2 red onion or 2 spring onions finely sliced
1 fresh lemon

Spike Smilgin
St Leonards-on-Sea

Boil the potatoes until cooked, remove and allow to cool.
Hardboil the eggs then plunge into cold water and allow to cool before shelling and cutting into quarters.
Steam (over the potatoes and eggs) or roast the green beans briefly until just cooked then cool in iced water.
Drain and dry with kitchen paper.
Remove skins from mackerel and break into largeish bite sized pieces
To assemble:
In a large bowl put potatoes, mackerel, herbs, capers, onions and dressing and lightly mix together with your fingers.
Arrange on a large flat or shallow platter.
Scatter with green beans and anchovies (removed from the oil), egg quarters and lemon cut into wedges, and serve with a salad of crisp mixed green leaves and some crusty bread.

58

SPRATS

500-700gm SPRATS
for family of 4
or more if your kids
are older
or for adults.
Flour
Salt & pepper
Oil for cooking

You eat the lot as
they are small -
like slightly bigger
whitebait – so no
bone problems
you just cook them
crunchy!

CHEAP, EASY & HEALTHY KIDS TEA.
Sprats are available in late winter and I
buy loads when I see them, wash & flour
them, lay them out flat in the freezer, then
bag them up when frozen. I then have
them available for last-minute healthy
meals when the kids arrive. I cook them
straight from frozen.

Put couple of tbsp of flour and salt &
pepper in a bowl.
Wash sprats to remove scales - you can
get the kids to do this...
If sprats are large and the eyes bother
you or the kids ... cut the heads off (the
sprats, not the kids...) roughly cleaning
out 'innards' as you go.
Otherwise, leave them whole.
Dry on kitchen paper.
Put in a bowl of flour and toss them
around a bit until they are covered.
Fry on medium heat in a bit of oil, turning
half way through.
Or cook them the way we prefer to cook
ours in hot oven, packed tightly side by
side, but top to tail so they fit better, in a
little oil, with a drizzle of oil on top.
15-20 mins at about 180°C fan. If you
want them crispier, turn halfway through.
Kids love them in pitas, with some

Marianne Smith coleslaw or grated carrots and ketchup.
Hastings Old Town Bon appetit.

59

Top chef **TOM AIKENS** gave a live cookery demonstration at the *Hastings Seafood & Wine Festival* on the Stade in 2008 and when we asked he immediately contributed recipes plus his top fish tips to our book. *Thanks Tom!*

HUSS WITH APPLE AND POTATO SALAD

Serves four
4 x 200g
HUSS FILLETS
75ml olive oil
2g lemon thyme leaves
2g chopped tarragon
30g butter
Juice of half a lemon
2g coarse sea salt
8 turns fresh
black pepper

Mix all the above together, brush this onto the huss fillets, season each fillet with salt and pepper and put a non-stick sauté pan onto heat with 50ml olive oil.
Carefully add the huss fillets and cook for 3-4 minutes.
Add the butter then flip over with a spatula and cook the other side for two minutes. Finish with a squeeze of lemon.

FOR THE SALAD
1 bunch of watercress
picked and washed
12g of tarragon leaves
2 Granny Smiths or
Braeburn apples

Apples washed and cut into thin slices and then a julienne on a Japanese mandolin. Toss in a little lemon juice to stop them from browning.

DRESSING FOR
THE SALAD
AND POTATOES
15g Dijon mustard
30g grain mustard
10g sugar
30g honey
120ml apple cider
vinegar
300ml vegetable oil
100ml olive oil
2g chopped tarragon
2g salt
8 turns fresh
black pepper

In a bowl whisk the mustard, vinegar, lemon juice, sugar, honey, salt and pepper together, and then slowly add the oils till emulsified, adding the tarragon last.

CHARLOTTE POTATOES
300g washed and scrubbed Charlotte potatoes
20g salt
8 tarragon sprigs
4 cloves of garlic cut in half
1.5 litre cold water

Place the potatoes, tarragon sprigs, and garlic in a pan with the cold water and slowly bring to a simmer, cook for 20 minutes till just tender depending on the size. When almost cooked take them off the heat and leave to cool at room temperature. Drain and leave to dry. Cut into 4mm thick slices.

TO FINISH THE POTATOES
2 spring onions peeled and finely sliced
2 tbsp chopped chives and tarragon
Sea salt and pepper
Dressing to bind the potatoes

Mix all the ingredients carefully with the potatoes and season with salt and pepper.

Tom Aikens
Chef

To Finish The Dish
Place the potato salad on the plate first, then follow with the fish on top, toss the watercress salad with the fine cut apple and some of the dressing, place on top or around the fish. Finally, drizzle some of the dressing over the huss and serve.

GURNARD WITH ORANGE AND LEMON
IN A PAPER BAG

SERVES FOUR
4 x 400g GURNARD,
scaled and gutted
(or *SEA BASS*,
***RED MULLET*,**
***SEA TROUT*)**
2 lemons and 1 orange
washed and the peel
removed with a
vegetable peeler and
left in large strips
Juice of 1 orange
100ml olive oil
40g unsalted butter
4g fresh lemon
thyme leaves
8 bay leaves cut into
quarters
4 sprigs of rosemary
4g coarse sea salt
10 turns of fresh
black pepper
1/2 bunch dill
1 x 24" square of
parchment paper

Tom Aikens
Chef

Take each whole gurnard, lie it on its side and make 4 slashes down each side and rub in the olive oil, butter, salt and pepper. Put the thyme leaves, rosemary and quartered bay leaves inside the slashes. Open the bellies and use half the strips of peel and dill to fill them. Take a square of paper and rub with olive oil. Place 1/4 of the remaining peel and dill on each one, just off centre, place a gurnard on top then drizzle the fish with orange juice and a little lemon juice. Carefully fold the paper over to the other side and secure with paper clips or staples. It should look like a little rectangle with the fish inside. Place the parcels on a baking tray and bake for 12-16 minutes at 180°C (Gas 4) and when you tear open the paper be careful of the steam coming out.
It will smell amazing.

WHITEBAIT CAKES

500g WHITEBAIT
2 or 3 large tomatoes,
finely chopped
1 large onion,
finely chopped
1 tsp mixed herbs
of your choice
1 tsp of chopped mint
Salt and pepper
Flour for binding

Artist Peter Waldron and his wife Lois divide their lives between Hastings Old Town and a small village in Crete. Their recipe has a distinctly Grecian flavour and as a bonus it looks hilarious!

Mix together the tomatoes, onion, herbs, mint and salt and pepper in a bowl.
Add some flour to the mixture and knead it together until not too runny.
Add the whitebait and mix well.
Heat olive oil in a frying pan and add a spoonful at a time. Cook for about 3 or 4 minutes on both sides, until golden brown.
Serve with lemon wedges
You will end up with fish cakes with the whitebait heads and tails sticking out all over the place!!

Peter & Lois Waldron

POACHED MACKEREL
WITH A MINTED HOLLANDAISE.

Serves 4
8 x fillets of fresh
MACKEREL
Mint for garnish
For the sauce:
2 tbsp sherry vinegar
1 shallot
finely chopped
2 tbsp cold water
2 free range
egg yolks
225g clarified butter
1 tsp lemon juice
good pinch of
cayenne pepper
1-2 tbsp chopped mint
(depends on your taste
and strength of mint)
Salt
freshly ground
black pepper.

Tony Howard
chef and
professional gardener,
Hastings Old Town

1. Make the sauce first. Put the sherry vinegar and shallot in a small pan and bring to the boil, reduce to about 1 tsp.
2. Half fill a pan with water and bring to the boil, lower to simmer then rest a glass bowl on top.
3. Put the water, egg yolks and sherry/shallot reduction into the bowl and whisk until light and fluffy.
4. Remove the bowl from the pan and slowly whisk in the butter, adding it very slowly, just like making a mayonnaise.
5. Add the lemon juice, cayenne pepper, chopped mint and some salt and pepper.
6. Set aside and keep warm in a bigger bowl of warm water.
7. Bring 1.5 litres (2 pints) of water and 2 tbsp of salt to the boil in a large flat pan, reduce to simmer, add mackerel and poach for 3 mins turning them over half way through the cooking.
8. Lift out drain well and serve two per person on a warm plate.
9. Spoon a little of the sauce over and the rest around the mackerel.
10. Garnish with a nice sprig of fresh mint.

64

WILD SALMON
COOKED IN CLINGFILM

4 FILLETS OF WILD
SCOTTISH SALMON
4 large
banana shallots
500g fresh garden
peas
250g diced pancetta
3 sticks celery
15g fresh basil
15g fresh flat leaf
Parsley
10g fresh dill
Lemon
Olive oil
Sea Salt and freshly
ground black pepper
Watercress
Clingfilm

Ben Krikorian

Wild salmon is not likely to be caught around these parts but it is delicious. It can be bought at Rock-a-Nore and this dish is served at The Dragon Bar in George Street.

Lay 30cm of clingfilm on a flat surface. Drizzle some olive oil on to the clingfilm with a pinch of sea salt and black pepper.

Lay your fresh herbs on the oil and place your salmon fillet on top.

Fold the clingfilm until you have a parcel with the herbs on the outside of the fillet.

Boil a large pan of water and turn down the heat until it simmers.

Add your fillets in the clingfilm to the water and simmer for 7-8 minutes.

Meanwhile, dice the celery, shallots and pancetta and saute in butter for 3 minutes add your peas and a splash of white wine and saute for a further 2 minutes.

Remove the salmon from the water and unwrap the clingfilm. To serve, place the salmon fillet on top of the pancetta mix and finish with a drizzle of lemon oil and a clump of watercress.

Sardines

SCRIBBLE PAGE

66

MY FAVOURITE DISHES & COOK'S NOTES

MY FAVOURITE DISHES & COOK'S NOTES

69

BREAD & OTHER PROVISIONS

JUDGES BAKERY
Award winning organic bakery
& so much more...
51 High Street
Hastings TN34 3EN
01424-722588
info@judgesbakery.com
www.judgesbakery.com

TRINITY WHOLEFOODS
Good for herbs, spices,
Oriental goodies and fresh veg
& Judges baked goods
3 Trinity Street
Hastings TN34 1HG
01424 430473

PLENTY
Provisions, Lighthouse Bakery's
bread, local ice cream
and fruit & veg
16 Grand Parade
St Leonards TN37 6DN
01424 439736
goods@plentyprovisions.co.uk
www.plentyprovisions.co.uk

WINCHELSEA FARM KITCHEN
Butchers, delicatessen, cheese,
wine, provisions & café.
11-12 High Street
Winchelsea
East Sussex TN36 4EA
01797 226287

WAKEHAMS FARM SHOP
Popular farm shop plus
plant nursery in summer
Pett Level Road
Fairlight East Sussex TN35 4ED
01424 814898

THE FISHMONGERS

ARCADE FISHERIES
Fresh fish daily
in the Town Centre
13 Queen's Arcade
Hastings TN34 1TA
01424 435459

ROCK-A-NORE FISHERIES
Fresh fish, oysters, Scottish
salmon, smokers & curers
3 Rock-a-Nore Road
Fishmarket
Hastings TN34 3DW
01424 445425
www.rockanorefisheries.co.uk

RX Fisheries
Fresh fish daily
Rock-a-Nore Road
Hasting TN34 3DW
01424 445239

RYE BAY FISH
Fresh fish from the Rye Fleet
by the Bridge
New Road
RYE TN31 7LS
01797 222377

SUTTONS FISH SHOP
Quality provisions
Fresh fish daily
Sea Road
Winchelsea
East East Sussex
TN36 4LA
01797 226261

Sally & Stewart Walton have lived and worked in Hastings for almost 20 years and have written many books on crafts, design and decorating. Fanatical about food, this is their first cook book. The couple now both work with recycled materials, Stewart with wood (www.recyclingwood.org.uk) and Sally with fabric (www.carry-a-bag.com) Debi Angel came to Hastings via London for week-ends in Rye Harbour. She is primarily known as a successful launch magazine design director and is also a passionate artist who loves the pace and colour of life beside the sea. (www.debiangel.com)

© SEA SAW BOOKS
www.seasawbooks.co.uk

SEA SAW BOOKS WOULD LIKE TO THANK:
Stephanie Donaldson, Louise Bell, Ali Graham...
& all at Hastings Printing Company Ltd.